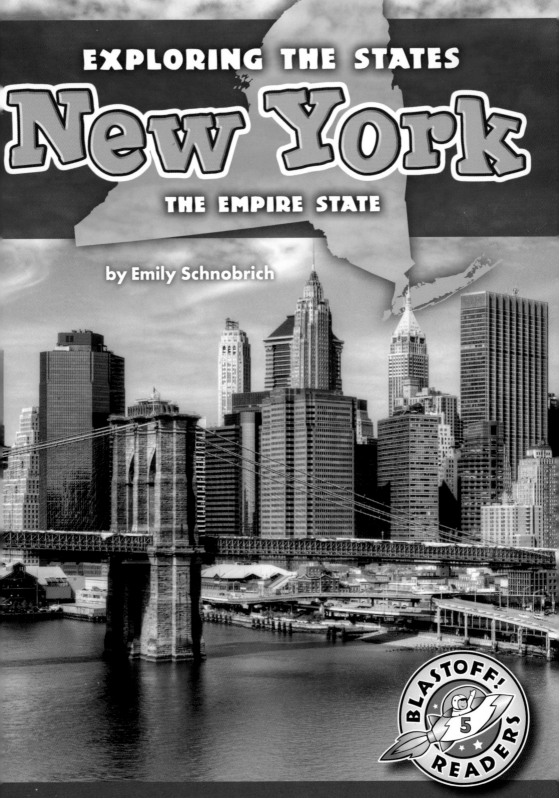

EXPLORING THE STATES

New York

THE EMPIRE STATE

by Emily Schnobrich

BELLWETHER MEDIA • MINNEAPOLIS, MN

Note to Librarians, Teachers, and Parents:

Blastoff! Readers are carefully developed by literacy experts and combine standards-based content with developmentally appropriate text.

Level 1 provides the most support through repetition of high-frequency words, light text, predictable sentence patterns, and strong visual support.

Level 2 offers early readers a bit more challenge through varied simple sentences, increased text load, and less repetition of high-frequency words.

Level 3 advances early-fluent readers toward fluency through increased text and concept load, less reliance on visuals, longer sentences, and more literary language.

Level 4 builds reading stamina by providing more text per page, increased use of punctuation, greater variation in sentence patterns, and increasingly challenging vocabulary.

Level 5 encourages children to move from "learning to read" to "reading to learn" by providing even more text, varied writing styles, and less familiar topics.

Whichever book is right for your reader, Blastoff! Readers are the perfect books to build confidence and encourage a love of reading that will last a lifetime!

This edition first published in 2014 by Bellwether Media, Inc.

No part of this publication may be reproduced in whole or in part without written permission of the publisher. For information regarding permission, write to Bellwether Media, Inc., Attention: Permissions Department, 5357 Penn Avenue South, Minneapolis, MN 55419.

Library of Congress Cataloging-in-Publication Data

Schnobrich, Emily.
 New York / by Emily Schnobrich.
    pages cm. – (Blastoff readers. Exploring the states)
 Includes bibliographical references and index.
 Summary: "Developed by literacy experts for students in grades three through seven, this book introduces young readers to the geography and culture of New York"–Provided by publisher.
 ISBN 978-1-62617-031-5 (hardcover : alk. paper)
 1. New York (State)–Juvenile literature. I. Title.
 F119.3.S35 2014
 974.7–dc23

                                                                                    2013007810

Printed in the United States of America, North Mankato, MN.

Table of Contents

Where Is New York?

New York lies in the northeastern corner of the United States. The St. Lawrence River forms part of its northern border with Canada. New York also borders two **Great Lakes**. Lake Ontario lies to the north, and Lake Erie is to the west. Vermont, Massachusetts, and Connecticut share New York's eastern border. New Jersey and Pennsylvania are its neighbors to the south.

New York's capital, Albany, stands on the banks of the Hudson River in the east. The state's southeastern tip includes Long Island and Staten Island. Bustling New York City stretches onto both.

Niagara
Falls

Buffalo

Lake
Erie

Canada

St. Lawrence River

Vermont

New
Hampshire

Lake
Ontario

● Rochester

Albany ★

Massachusetts

New York

Hudson River

Connecticut

Pennsylvania

New York City ●

Long
Island

Staten
Island

New
Jersey

Atlantic
Ocean

N
W · E
S

History

The Iroquois and Algonquin **Native** Americans lived in New York before Europeans arrived. In 1624, the Dutch became the first Europeans to settle the land. Later, important battles took place in New York during the **Revolutionary War**. By the late 1800s, New York was a center of business, transportation, and culture. It was already one of the most important places in the world.

Did you know?

Ellis Island was built in 1892 as an entry point to the United States. For a while, Ellis Island received more than 5,000 immigrants every day.

New York Timeline!

1609:	Henry Hudson is the first European to explore what will become New York.
1664:	The English arrive and take New York from the Dutch.
1763:	With help from the Iroquois, the English defeat France for control of New York.
1775-1783:	The colonies fight for independence in the Revolutionary War.
1788:	New York becomes the eleventh state.
1825:	The Erie Canal opens and encourages westward travel.
1848:	Seneca Falls hosts an important convention for women's rights.
1929:	The U.S. Stock Market crashes and the Great Depression begins.
2001:	Terrorists attack the World Trade Center towers in New York City.

Erie Canal

The Great Depression

World Trade Center attack

The Land

New York's Climate
average °F

spring
Low: 37°
High: 56°

summer
Low: 60°
High: 79°

fall
Low: 43°
High: 60°

winter
Low: 21°
High: 35°

Adirondack
Mountains

A variety of landscapes fill the state of New York. Rugged mountains, grassy **plains**, and rolling hills cover the state. The highest mountains are the Adirondacks in the northeast. The great Hudson River runs south near the eastern border. New York City sprawls at its **mouth**. The Hudson River Valley surrounds the river and city.

A collection of skinny lakes called the Finger Lakes lies in the west. Cows graze in the grassy valleys nearby. To the north and west, low plains line the borders of Lakes Ontario and Erie.

Whiteface

! fun fact

Whiteface Mountain is one of the highest peaks in the Adirondacks. Skiers enjoy the mountain because it has the steepest vertical drop east of the Rocky Mountains.

Niagara Falls

One of the world's largest waterfalls is in the northwestern corner of New York. Niagara Falls is a long, spectacular cliff of water. More than 500,000 gallons (1,892,705 liters) of water thunder over the falls every second. It could fill about 50 Olympic-size swimming pools in a minute!

The falls are surrounded by the oldest state park in the country. **Tourists** hike lush trails and bridges that cross the waters. At the Cave of Winds, people can walk within feet of the falls. The rushing water creates wet, windy conditions. Visitors wear rain gear to stay warm and dry.

Cave of Winds

fun fact !

Visitors can get a closer look at the falls on the Maid of the Mist. This boat tour is one of the oldest tourist attractions in America!

spotted salamander

fun fact !

The spotted salamander makes its home in the damp soil of New York's parks and forests. It can live up to twenty years!

Three-fifths of New York is covered in forests. Furry animals such as deer mice, red foxes, and snowshoe hares scurry through the woods. Bobcats, black bears, and coyotes live in mountain forests. Yellow buttercups and delicate wild roses grow underfoot.

buttercups

deer mouse

bobcat

White-tailed deer roam through fields of daisies and black-eyed Susans. **Migrating** birds such as Canada geese graze near lakes and ponds. Hunters search for grouse, wild turkeys, and other **game** birds. Sometimes majestic bald eagles soar overhead.

Landmarks

New York boasts plenty of state parks and natural beauty. The misty Adirondack Mountains are a popular destination. In fall, the peaks burst into fiery colors. In the winter, people ski at **resorts** near Lake Placid. The state's Finger Lakes region offers relaxing beaches and little towns to explore.

History fans like the museum at **Fort** Ticonderoga on Lake Champlain. In 1775, **colonists** captured the fort from the British. The National Baseball Hall of Fame in Cooperstown celebrates the history of America's favorite pastime. At beautiful Hyde Park, visitors can tour President Franklin D. Roosevelt's 35-room mansion.

Fort Ticonderoga

fun fact

Tourists like to ride to the top of the shimmering Empire State Building in Manhattan. At 1,250 feet (381 meters), it was the tallest building in the world for over 30 years.

Empire State Building

The Statue of Liberty in New York City was a gift from France. From head to toe, Lady Liberty is 112 feet (34 meters) tall.

New York City

Central Park

Did you know?

New York City is home to the United Nations Headquarters. This global organization works for peace between different countries.

New York City is the largest **metropolis** in the country. It includes five **boroughs**, or smaller cities. Most people live in apartments. They get around on buses or **subway** trains. New York City is made up of many different neighborhoods. Each has its own unique culture. Tiny shops sell dumplings in Chinatown. Bankers and business people go to work on **Wall Street**.

Wall Street

Chinatown

New York City is sometimes called "the city that never sleeps." There is always something happening. People picnic, jog, and ice skate in sprawling Central Park. Fashion lovers crowd fancy shops on Madison Avenue and Fifth Avenue. Students attend the city's more than 100 different colleges and universities.

New Yorkers make all sorts of things. Some people publish books and magazines. Others design and sew clothing. New Yorkers also build computer and electronic equipment. In the countryside, farmers raise cows for milk and beef. Others grow tomatoes, cabbages, sweet corn, and apples. Fishers pull in pounds of seafood from the Atlantic Ocean.

Most New Yorkers have **service jobs**. Many work at large **financial companies**. Others cook at restaurants, run theaters, and work at shops and hotels. New Yorkers must also manage airports, subways, bus systems, and waterways.

Where People Work in New York

manufacturing
5%

farming and
natural resources
1%

government
14%

services
80%

Playing

Yankees game

New Yorkers love to root for sports teams. Baseball fans cheer for the New York Yankees or Mets. The Knicks are the state's most famous basketball team. Outdoor adventurers hike and ski in the mountains. Coney Island features an amusement park and beaches. The Hamptons, a group of villages on Long Island, attracts sunbathers in summer.

American Museum of Natural History

New York City Marathon

fun fact

The New York City Marathon is the largest marathon in the world. The 26.2-mile (42.1-kilometer) route snakes through all five boroughs of the city.

In New York City, people attend orchestra concerts, ballets, and operas at the Lincoln Center for the Performing Arts. Nearby, the American Museum of Natural History features a life-size model of a blue whale.

Potato Latkes

Ingredients:

- 2 cups peeled and shredded potatoes
- 3 tablespoons grated onion
- 1 egg, beaten
- 2 tablespoons flour
- 1 teaspoon salt
- Oil for frying

Directions:

1. Wring out water from potatoes using a clean cheesecloth or paper towel. Stir potatoes, onion, eggs, flour, and salt together in a medium bowl.

2. Heat oil in a large, heavy skillet. Place large spoonfuls of potato mixture into hot oil, pressing them down to 1/4 to 1/2 inch patties.

3. Brown on one side, then flip and brown the other. Drain on paper towels.

4. Serve hot with applesauce or sour cream.

Russian dumplings

Buffalo wings

! fun fact

New Yorkers came up with some famous foods. Buffalo wings, Thousand Island dressing, and potato chips were all invented in New York.

New York is home to **immigrants** from all over the world. Almost every type of food can be found there. Near Brighton Beach in New York City, Russian restaurants sell dumplings filled with vegetables or meat. Jewish delis serve giant beef sandwiches and potato pancakes called *latkes*.

New Yorkers eat big slices of pizza that they can fold in half. They also love bagels topped with cream cheese and smoked salmon. Vendors sell sizzling hot dogs on the streets. In the countryside, New Yorkers tap maple trees for syrup and make apples into cider.

Festivals

New Yorkers celebrate many cultures. Red and gold dragons dance through Chinatown during the Lunar New Year Parade. Visitors experience Japanese culture at the Cherry Blossom Festival in Brooklyn. Millions of people line the streets to watch giant balloons float by in the Macy's Thanksgiving Day Parade.

Every spring, more than 100,000 tulips bloom at the Tulip Festival in Albany. Visitors to the National Buffalo Wing Festival compete in wild eating contests. Berry, apple, and pumpkin festivals are scattered across the state. Many cities also have their own art fairs, jazz concerts, and film festivals.

Lunar New Year Parade

Macy's Thanksgiving Day Parade

Years ago, theaters in New York City were clustered around Broadway Street. Broadway's trail of glowing theater lights was called "The Great White Way." Today, the word *Broadway* makes people think of the best theater in America. It is one of the reasons why millions of tourists visit New York every year.

There are currently 40 Broadway theaters in New York City. Most of them are near crowded Times Square. This block of stores is full of giant **billboards** and honking yellow taxis. Broadway represents the glitter and opportunity of New York City. It is one of many symbols of the Empire State's **diversity** and charm.

fun fact

The longest-running Broadway show is *The Phantom of the Opera*. Actors have performed the musical more than 10,000 times!

Fast Facts About New York

New York's Flag

New York's flag is dark blue with a coat of arms in the center. The coat of arms features an image of the sun rising over the Hudson River. An eagle is perched on a small globe above it. Two women stand beside the coat of arms. They represent Liberty and Justice. Beneath the coat of arms is a white ribbon that bears the state motto.

State Flower
rose

State Nickname:	The Empire State
State Motto:	*Excelsior*; "Ever Upward"
Year of Statehood:	1788
Capital City:	Albany
Other Major Cities:	New York City, Buffalo, Rochester
Population:	19,378,102 (2010)
Area:	53,095 square miles (137,515 square kilometers); New York is the 27th largest state.
Major Industries:	services, manufacturing, farming, publishing, fashion
Natural Resources:	stone, salt, sand, gravel
State Government:	150 representatives; 62 senators
Federal Government:	27 representatives; 2 senators
Electoral Votes:	29

State Animal
beaver

State Bird
eastern bluebird

29

Glossary

billboards—large outdoor screens or boards that advertise products or businesses

boroughs—the five sections of New York City; they are The Bronx, Brooklyn, Manhattan, Queens, and Staten Island.

colonists—people who settle new land for their home country

diversity—variety of cultures or backgrounds

financial companies—companies that assist people and businesses in managing money

fort—a strong building made to protect lands; forts are often occupied by troops and surrounded by other defenses.

game—wild animals that are hunted for food or sport

Great Lakes—five large freshwater lakes on the border between the United States and Canada

immigrants—people who leave one country to live in another country

metropolis—a large, busy city

migrating—traveling from one place to another, often with the seasons

mouth—the place where a river or stream empties into a larger body of water

native—originally from a specific place

plains—large areas of flat land

resorts—vacation spots that offer recreation, entertainment, and relaxation

Revolutionary War—the war between 1775 and 1783 in which the United States fought for independence from Great Britain

service jobs—jobs that perform tasks for people or businesses

subway—an underground railway that runs through big cities

tourists—people who travel to visit another place

Wall Street—a street in New York City where many large financial companies do business

To Learn More

AT THE LIBRARY

MacPhail Knight, Joan. *Charlotte in New York*. San Francisco, Calif.: Chronicle Books, 2006.

Platt, Richard. *Through Time: New York City*. New York, N.Y.: Kingfisher, 2010.

Santella, Andrew. *Building the New York Subway*. New York, N.Y.: Children's Press, 2007.

ON THE WEB

Learning more about New York is as easy as 1, 2, 3.

1. Go to www.factsurfer.com.

2. Enter "New York" into the search box.

3. Click the "Surf" button and you will see a list of related Web sites.

With factsurfer.com, finding more information is just a click away.

Index

The images in this book are reproduced through the courtesy of: SeanPavonePhoto, front cover (bottom), p. 17 (top); BAO/ Glow Images, p. 6; ClassicStock.com/ SuperStock, p. 7 (left); CSU Archive/ Age Fotostock, p. 7 (middle); Ken Tannenbaum, p. 7 (right); Colin D. Young, pp. 8-9; Wangkun Jia, p. 9; Anne Kitzman, p. 10 (top); ValeStock, p. 10 (bottom); MountainHardcore, pp. 10-11; Matt Jeppson, pp. 12-13; Adam Rauso, p. 13 (top); StevenRussellSmithPhotos, p. 13 (middle); Geoffrey Kuchera, p. 13 (bottom); Jeffery M. Frank, p. 14 (top); Marc Venema, p. 14 (bottom); Kropic1, pp. 14-15; Stuart Monk, pp. 16-17; Peeter Viisimaa, p. 17 (bottom); CandyBox Images, p. 18; Anna Bryukhanova, p. 19; Gary Yim, pp. 20-21; Jorg Hackemann, p. 21 (top); Steve Broer, p. 21 (bottom); Lisa F. Young, p. 22; Wiktory, p. 23; Igor Dutina, p. 23 (small); Joshua Haviv, p. 24 (small); Gary718, pp. 24-25; Andrey Bayda, pp. 26-27; Infusny-236/ Walter McBride/ INFphoto.com/ Newscom, p. 27 (small); Pakmor, p. 28 (top); Hong Vo, p. 28 (bottom); Steve Byland, p. 29 (left); Ammit Jack, p. 29 (right).